The Best of SHORTIES

2nd B♭ Trumpet

Arranged by VICTOR LÓPEZ

An All-Purpose Marching Band/Pep Band Book for Stands, Time-Outs,
Pep Rallies and a Host of Other Uses

THE BEST OF SHORTIES

Fourteen Super Pop Arrangements plus "The Star-Spangled Banner" and "Happy Birthday"

Arranged by VICTOR LÓPEZ

3.
"Louie, Louie"
By RICHARD BERRY

Bright rock
div.
mf
f
div.
mf
f
ff

4.
"Shout"
By O'KELLY ISLEY, RONALD ISLEY and RUDOLPH ISLEY

Bright gospel rock
div.
f
f
f
cresc. poco a poco
ff

"Rock Around The Clock"
5.
By MAX C. FREEDMAN and JIMMY DE KNIGHT
Swing Style
div.
f
"In-A-Gadda-Da-Vida"
6.
By DOUG INGLE
Moderate Rock
f

7.
"Wipe Out"
By THE SURFARIS

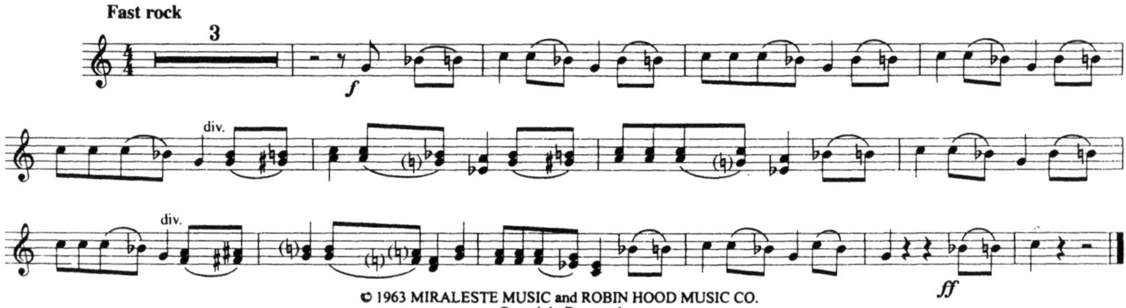

Fast rock
3
f
div.
div.
ff

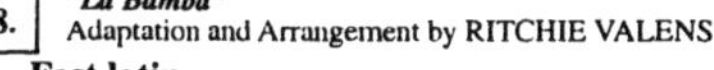

8.
"La Bamba"
Adaptation and Arrangement by RITCHIE VALENS
Fast latin

div.
f
V   V
V   V
div.
div.
3   3
div.
f   cresc.   ff   fff

9. *"Tequila"*
By CHUCK RIO

Latin rock

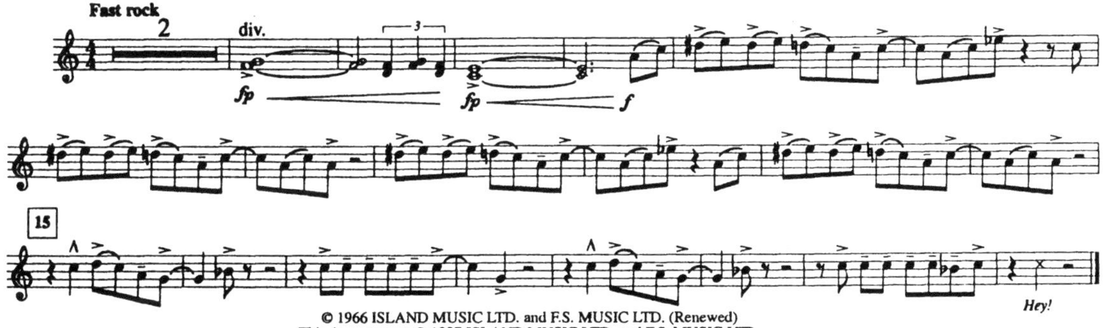

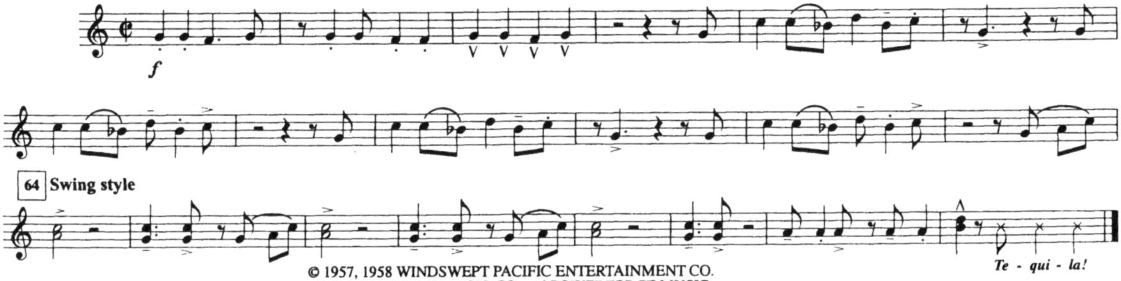
64 Swing style
Te - qui - la!

10. *"Gimme Some Lovin'"*
By STEVE WINWOOD, MUFF WINWOOD
and SPENCER DAVIS

Fast rock

div.
15
Hey!

11. *"That's The Way (I Like It)"*
Words and Music by HARRY CASEY and RICHARD FINCH

Moderately

12. *"Land Of A Thousand Dances"*
Words and Music by CHRIS KENNER

Bright rock

13. *"Soul Man"*
Words and Music by ISAAC HAYES and DAVID PORTER

Medium funk

© 1968 WALDEN MUSIC, INC. and ALMO MUSIC CORP.
All Rights Administered by WB MUSIC CORP.
This Arrangement © 1998 WALDEN MUSIC, INC. and ALMO MUSIC CORP.
All Rights Reserved

14. *"Your Mama Don't Dance"*
Words and Music by JIM MESSINA and KENNY LOGGINS

Rock shuffle

© 1972 JASPERILLA MUSIC CO. and WINGATE MUSIC CORP.
All Rights Administered by ALMO MUSIC CORP.
This Arrangement © 1998 JASPERILLA MUSIC CO. and WINGATE MUSIC CORP.
All Rights Reserved

MBFM00008

15. *"Bad To The Bone"*
Words and Music by GEORGE THOROGOOD

Moderate shuffle

16. *"Bang The Drum All Day"*
Words and Music by TODD RUNDGREN

Bright rock

MBFM00008